Donated in memory of
Wilton Hunter Talley &
Elizabeth Almond Talley
by Julia Talley Draucker
January, 1993

Riddles and More Riddles

compiled by J. Michael Shannon

illustrated by Diana L. Magnuson

created by The Child's World

CHILDRENS PRESS, CHICAGO

Library of Congress Cataloging in Publication Data

Shannon, J. Michael.
   Riddles and more riddles.

   (Laughing matters)
   Summary: A compilation of riddles from ancient times
to the present. Includes instructions on making up
your own riddles.
   1. Riddles, Juvenile. [1. Riddles] I. Magnuson,
Diana, ill. II. Series.
PN6371.5.S53   1983   398'.6   82-19765
ISBN 0-516-01873-6

Copyright© 1983 by Regensteiner Publishing Enterprises, Inc.
All rights reserved. Published simultaneously in Canada.
Printed in the United States of America.
          7 8 9 10 R 92 91 90

TABLE OF CONTENTS

Riddles Through the Years 4

Riddles About Science 8

Riddles About Math 12

Riddles About Famous People 16

Riddles About States 20

Riddles About Children 23

Riddles About Animals 28

Riddles From Many Countries 34

More Riddles 37

New Riddles 42

Write Your Own Riddles 45

Through the Years

Have you ever told, or heard a riddle? If you have, you are in good company. Riddles have been around a long time and have been popular with people of all ages.

One of the oldest riddles comes to us from ancient Greece. It tells us of the legend of the sphinx. According to the story, the sphinx told people to answer her riddle or die. Many tried, but no one could answer the sphinx's riddle. Then a man named Oedipus guessed right. Below is the riddle of the sphinx.

"What has one voice but walks on four legs in the morning, two legs in the afternoon, and three legs at night?"

What do you think? Would you have made it past the sphinx? Oedipus' answer was: "man." In the riddle, the morning stands for when one is a child and crawls on all fours. The afternoon stands for the adult who walks on two feet. The evening stands for old age, when one walks with the help of a cane. (Using a cane is like walking on three legs.)

You can see why so many people could not answer the riddle. (By the way, according to the story, when Oedipus gave the right answer, the sphinx got so upset, *she* died.)

There is also a riddle in the Bible. It was told by Samson to the men at his wedding party. On the way to the party, Samson saw a lion he had killed. Some bees had made a hive in the lion. When he saw honey in the lion, it gave him an idea for a riddle.

"Out of the eater came something to eat. Out of the strong came something sweet."

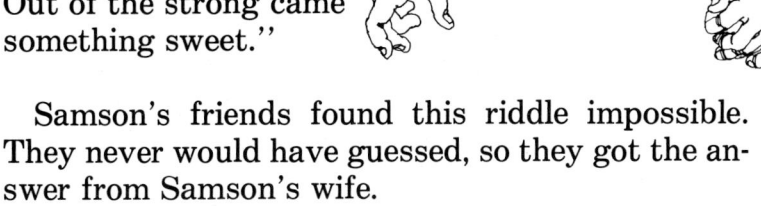

Samson's friends found this riddle impossible. They never would have guessed, so they got the answer from Samson's wife.

5

Mystery riddles were popular all the way up to the 1700s, and are still around today. In fact, many of our nursery rhymes, such as "Humpty Dumpty" and "Rock-A-Bye Baby," were originally considered riddles. We know now that Humpty Dumpty was an egg, because that was the answer to the riddle. In "Rock-A-Bye Baby," the baby and cradle are a bird in its nest.

Here is one of the popular nursery rhyme riddles of the past:

Little Nancy Etticoat
In her white petticoat
With a red nose—
The longer she stands
The shorter she grows.

What is "she"?

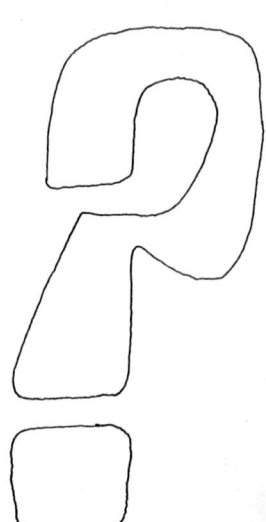

A candle.

History tells us Abe Lincoln used riddles in some of his debates. Once Lincoln felt his opponent was ignoring the facts, so he asked:

"How many legs does a mule have if you call a tail a leg?"

The answer is four. Calling a tail a leg doesn't make it a leg.

So you see, besides being funny, a riddle can teach a lesson.

Most riddles today make use of puns or some other kind of play on words to make their point. They usually use words that sound alike or have more than one meaning.

Whether they are jokes or puzzles, riddles are meant for fun today. So go ahead, have fun!

About Science

1. Why did the scientist install a knocker on his door?
2. What is the deepest part of the Atlantic Ocean?
3. Which is faster, heat or cold?
4. When will water stop flowing over a waterfall?
5. What holds the moon in its orbit?
6. Why do clocks slow down?
7. When can't astronauts go to the moon?
8. Why is electricity so dangerous?

Answers:

1. He wanted to win the no-bell prize.
2. The bottom.
3. Heat—it's easy to catch cold.
4. When it reaches the bottom.
5. Moon beams.
6. Because they have to run all day.
7. When it is full.
8. Because it doesn't know how to conduct itself.

1. Why are weather forecasters so absent-minded?
2. What gets wetter the longer it dries?
3. What color gets noticed the most?
4. When does the ocean roar the loudest?
5. Why was the wheel such an important invention?
6. Why do so many people want to be astronomers?

Answers:

1. Their heads are always in the clouds.
2. A towel.
3. A loud color.
4. When there are crabs in its bed.
5. It got everything else going.
6. Their business is always looking up.

9

1. What is light as a feather, but can't be held for more than a couple of minutes?
2. What kind of candy bar can you find in space?
3. What do you get when you cross a duck with a roadrunner?
4. What do you get when you cross a turtle with a parrot?
5. What happens when you cross a chicken and a dog?
6. What stars should you stay away from?

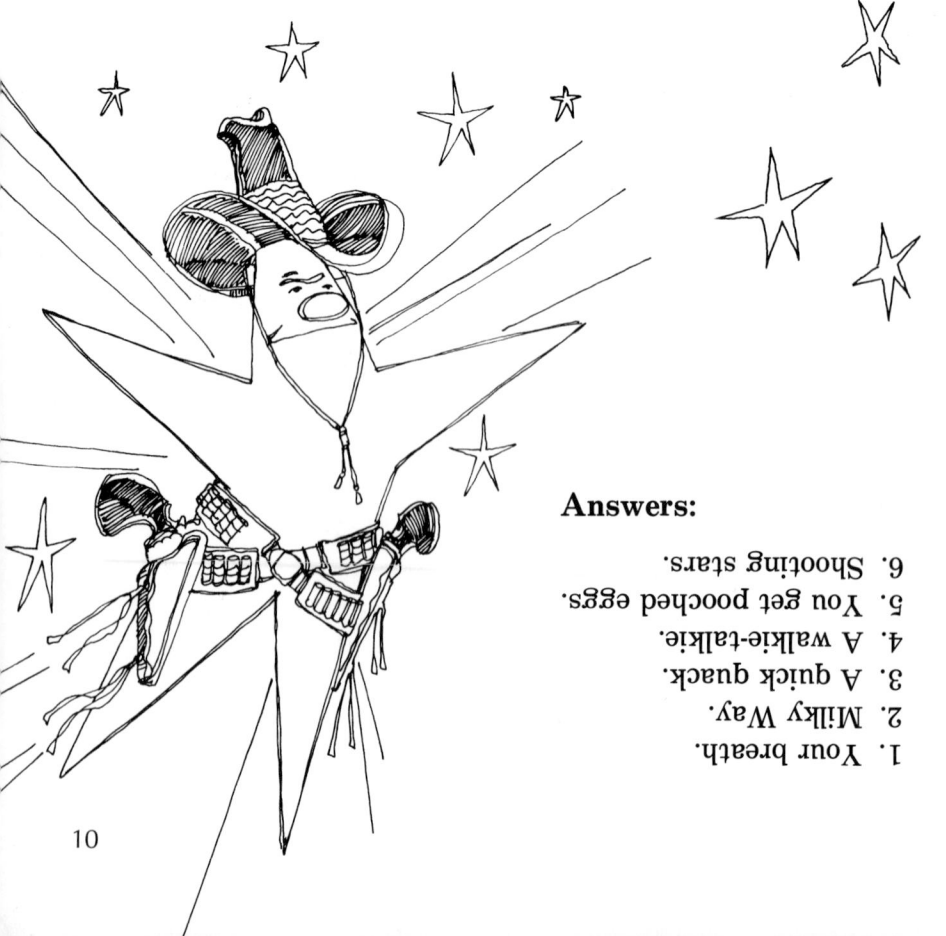

Answers:
1. Your breath.
2. Milky Way.
3. A quick quack.
4. A walkie-talkie.
5. You get pooched eggs.
6. Shooting stars.

1. If we breathe oxygen in the morning, what do we breathe in the evening?
2. What tree can you carry in your hand?
3. How much dirt can you take out of a hole three feet by three feet?
4. How much water can you put in an empty glass?
5. If athletes get athlete's foot, what do astronauts get?
6. Why do scientists study noses?
7. What's the fastest plant?

Answers:

1. Nite-ro-gen.
2. Palm.
3. None. The dirt has already been taken out.
4. None. It wouldn't be empty.
5. Missile toe.
6. To see what makes them run.
7. A running vine.

About Math

1. Why did the boy take his math book to the doctor?
2. Why did the mathematician love his calculator?
3. How can you drop an egg six feet without breaking it?
4. How is the number nine like a peacock?
5. How do you divide five potatoes equally between three people?
6. How can you jump off of a 40-foot ladder and not get hurt?
7. When do two and two not make four?

Answers:

1. Because it had so many problems.
2. Because he could always count on it.
3. Drop it seven feet and it will fall six feet without breaking.
4. Without its tail it's nothing.
5. Mash them.
6. Jump off of the bottom rung.
7. When they make 22.

1. What's ten plus five minus fifteen?
    three plus six minus nine?
    seventeen plus three minus twenty?
2. What kind of table did the mathematician buy?
3. What number increases in value when it's turned upside down?
4. What number can you take half from and leave nothing?
5. How many feet are there in a yard?
6. How many months have 28 days?

Answers:

1. A lot of work for nothing.
2. A multiplication table.
3. Six (6).
4. Eight (8).
5. It depends on the number of people standing in it.
6. All of them.

1. What's the easiest way to double your money?
2. How many times can you subtract 10 from 100?
3. When is a mathematician like a snake?
4. What is a forum?
5. What is invisible yet you can measure it?
6. What animals are best at math?

Answers:

1. Fold it.
2. Once. After the first time it wouldn't be 100.
3. When he is an adder.
4. A two-um plus a two-um.
5. Your temperature.
6. Rabbits. They multiply quickly.

1. As I was going to St. Ives
   I met a man with seven wives
   Each wife had seven sacks
   Each sack had seven cats
   Each cat had seven kits.
   How many were going to St. Ives?
2. What's the difference between twice twenty and two, and twice two and twenty?
3. Why is a dollar smarter than a quarter?
4. If a farmer had two dozen sheep, and all but eleven ran away, how many does he have left?
5. How is two plus two equals five like your left hand?
6. What can you count on no matter what?
7. What has three feet but no legs?

Answers:

1. One.
2. One is 42, and the other is 24.
3. It has more cents.
4. Eleven.
5. Neither one is right.
6. Your fingers.
7. A yardstick.

15

About Famous People

1. Why did Betsy Ross volunteer to make a flag?

2. Where did King Arthur learn to joust?
3. Why did people have trouble finding Abe Lincoln in Washington, D.C.?
4. Where is George Washington buried?
5. What did people think of the Wright brothers?

Answers:

1. Because it was sew easy.
2. In knight school.
3. They had his Gettysburg Address.
4. In the ground.
5. They thought the Wrights were plane crazy.

1. What did Ben Franklin say when he discovered electricity?
2. What happened on Caesar's 39th birthday?
3. What did Paul Revere say at the end of his famous ride?
4. Where was Solomon's temple?
5. Why did Theodore Roosevelt use up so many horses?
6. How are Walter Cronkite and a plate of french fries alike?

Answers:

1. "I'm shocked."
2. He turned 39.
3. "Whoa!"
4. On his head.
5. Because he was a rough rider.
6. They used to be common taters.

1. What's the first thing Thomas Jefferson did each morning?
2. Why was Jonah so moody?
3. How do we know that Jesse James was strong?
4. Why did Robin Hood steal from the rich and give to the poor?
5. Where was Henry VIII crowned?
6. Why did Hank Aaron make so much money as a baseball player?
7. How was one Roman emperor like the letter P?
8. What bus ran from Spain to America?

Answers:

1. He woke up.
2. Because he spent so much time down in the mouth.
3. He used to hold up trains.
4. Because it wouldn't work the other way around.
5. On his head.
6. A good batter always makes good dough.
7. He was Nero (near o).
8. Columbus.

1. When was Adam born?
2. How did Alexander Graham Bell invent the telephone?
3. Why did Ben Franklin believe that the United States would be a healthy country?
4. How did Shakespeare manage to write so many plays?
5. When was Dr. Jekyll hard to find?
6. What president had the largest family?

Answers:

1. A little before Eve.
2. He had good connections.
3. He knew it had a good constitution.
4. He had Will power.
5. When he became Mr. Hyde.
6. George Washington. He was the father of the country.

19

About States

1. What did Ida ho?
2. How did Flora die? (Florida)
3. What did Dela ware?
4. What did I.O. weigh? (Iowa)
5. Why did Cali phone ya? (California)

Answers:

1. She hoed her Mary land.
2. She died in Misery (Missouri).
3. She wore a New Jersey.
4. She weighed a Washing ton.
5. He called to say, "How ah ya?" (Hawaii)

1. Where has Ore gone?
2. What did Tenne see?
3. What did Missi sip?
4. Did Wiscon sin?
5. What state is high in the middle and round on both ends?
6. What did Ohi-o?
7. What is the happiest state?
8. Why did so many people move to Missouri?

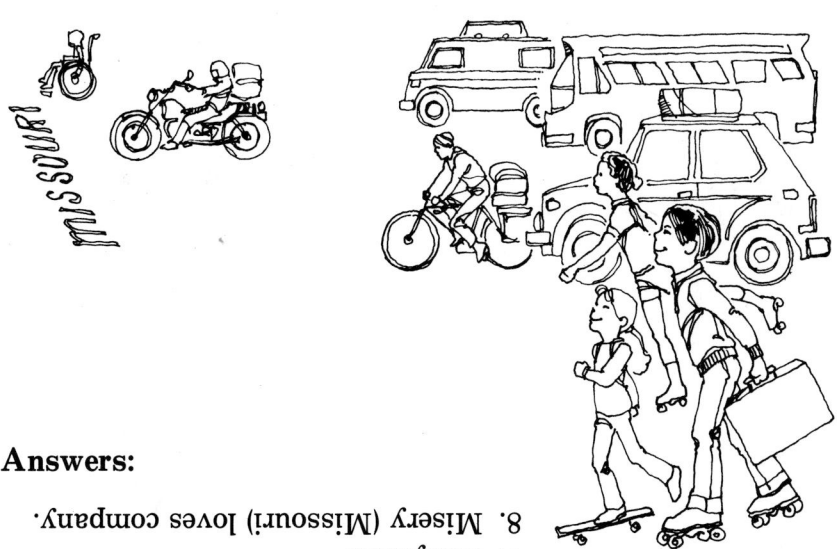

Answers:

1. She's gone to Okla homa.
2. An Arkan saw.
3. She sipped a Mini soda (Minnesota).
4. I don't know, but Al aska.
5. O hi O.
6. He owed his Taxes (Texas).
7. Maryland.
8. Misery (Missouri!) loves company.

21

1. What has four eyes but cannot see?
2. What was the largest moving job ever attempted?
3. What was the largest plumbing job ever attempted?
4. Do you know what old Ken took? (Kentucky)
5. What's the largest pencil in the world?

Answers:

5. Pennsylvania.
4. He took a new brass key (Nebraska).
3. Flushing, Michigan.
2. Wheeling, West Virginia.
1. Mississippi.

About Children

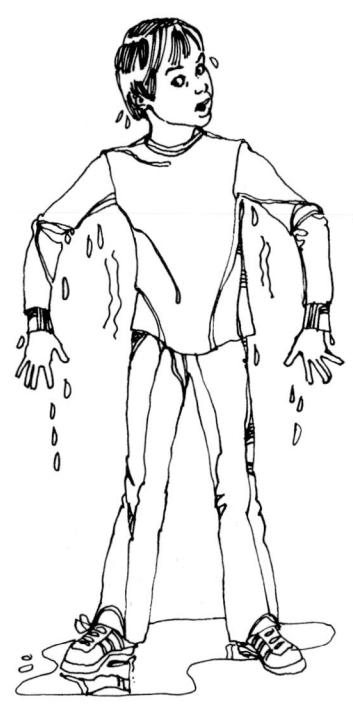

1. Why did the boy put on a wet shirt?
2. Why did the boy put his bed in the fireplace?
3. What did the girl do when her dog started chewing her dictionary?
4. Why did the boy sit on the stove?
5. Why did the girl stand on her head at the beach?

Answers:
1. Because the label said, "wash and wear."
2. He wanted to sleep like a log.
3. She took the words right out of his mouth.
4. He wanted to ride the range.
5. She wanted to put a wave in her hair.

1. Why did the girl leave her purse open outside?
2. Why did the boy think that all kings were 12-inches tall?

3. Why did the boy throw lettuce in the air?
4. Why did the girl put firecrackers in her hair?

Answers:

1. She heard there would be some change in the weather.
2. Because he heard that all kings were rulers.
3. He wanted to make a tossed salad.
4. So she could wear bangs.

1. Why did the girl mix up yeast and shoe polish?

2. Why should babies be allowed to cry?
3. Why did the boy cut down the tree?
4. What happened when the boy yelled through the screen door?

Answers:

1. She wanted to rise and shine.
2. If they didn't, they'd get back-tear-ia.
3. It was knotty (naughty).
4. He strained his voice.

1. Where do you put crying children?
2. Why do farmers never let their children around the chickens?
3. Why did the boy put his father in the refrigerator?
4. How do children grow?
5. Why did the girl close the refrigerator door?
6. What did the little boy say when his puppy ran away?

Answers:

1. In a bawl park.
2. Because chickens use fowl language.
3. He wanted a cold pop.
4. In a kindergarten.
5. Because she saw the salad dressing.
6. "Dog gone."

1. What is the child of a cannonball called?

2. Why did the mother knit three socks for her son?
3. Why did the boy hit his hand with the hammer?
4. Who is bigger, Mrs. Bigger or her baby girl?
5. What does a little ear of corn call his father?
6. Why did the girl take up tennis?
7. Why did the girl put money in the freezer?

Answers:

1. A BB.
2. He had grown another foot.
3. He wanted to be a swell guy.
4. Her baby is a little Bigger.
5. Popcorn.
6. She wanted to raise a racket (racquet).
7. So she could get some cold, hard cash.

About Animals

1. What did the dog say when the boy pulled his tail?
2. Why do hummingbirds hum?
3. What happens when birds fly upside down?
4. What kind of horse never goes out in the daytime?
5. What is the snake's favorite holiday?
6. What is black and white and red all over?
7. How do you keep an elephant from charging?

Answers:
1. "This is the end of me."
2. They can't remember the words.
3. They quack up.
4. A night mare.
5. Fangs-giving.
6. An embarrassed penguin.
7. Cancel his credit card.

1. How do you calm a fire-breathing dragon?
2. Why was the rabbit honored?
3. What did the rabbit say to the carrot?
4. Why did the baseball team hire a frog?
5. What do you get when you cross a porcupine with a cactus?
6. What did the apple say to the worm?

Answers:

1. Throw some water on him and he'll let off steam.
2. Because he was a hero in the hare-force.
3. "Nice gnawing you."
4. Because he never missed a fly.
5. Hurt.
6. "You bore me."

1. What are the largest ants in the world?
2. What are the second largest ants in the world?
3. Where do moths go to have fun?
4. What did the chicken say when it laid a square egg?
5. Why did the farmer give up keeping rabbits?
6. What kind of clothes does a dog wear?

Answers:
1. Gi-ants.
2. Eleph-ants.
3. A moth ball.
4. "Ouch."
5. Because it was a hare-raising experience.
6. Coat and pants.

1. Why did the rest of the animals keep secrets from the pig?
2. How can you tell when an owl is tired?
3. Why did the police arrest a bird?
4. What's the best year for a kangaroo?
5. Where do animals go when they lose their tails?

Answers:

1. Because he was a squealer.
2. He doesn't give a hoot.
3. Because he was a robin.
4. Leap year.
5. To a retail store.

1. Why did the chicken stop in the middle of the road?
2. What happened when the the firefly backed into the fan?
3. How is the tail of a dog like the inside of a tree?
4. Why can't pigs drive cars?
5. What did the bee say when he got home?

Answers:

1. She wanted to lay it on the line.
2. He was de-lighted.
3. They are both far away from the bark.
4. They would become road hogs.
5. "Hi, honey."

1. Where does a sheep get his wool cut?
2. What is the smartest kind of bee?
3. How do you fix a broken gorilla?
4. What was the bull doing behind the barn?
5. Why did the ants run across the cookie box?
6. What's a mosquito's favorite sport?

Answers:

1. At a baa baa shop.
2. A spelling bee.
3. With a monkey wrench.
4. Bulldozing.
5. It said, "Tear across the dotted line."
6. Skin diving.

From Many Countries

ARGENTINA
1. What animal has eight feet, six eyes, and a tail?

AFRICA
2. What teaches without talking?

PERSIA
3. What is all tongue?

PUERTO RICO
4. What can we swallow that can also swallow us?

Answers:

1. A horse with two riders.
2. A book.
3. Fire.
4. Water.

INDIA
1. What eats and drinks but cannot walk?
2. What can you see in the evening but is gone by morning?
3. What has a long tail, but isn't a squirrel, flies in the sky, but isn't a bird?

HUNGARY
4. What is both inside and outside a house?

Answers:

1. A tree. 2. Darkness. 3. A kite. 4. The front door.

SWEDEN
1. What is nothing but holes yet is strong?

WEST INDIES
2. What is hard like a rock, but isn't a rock, white like milk but isn't milk, sweet as sugar but isn't sugar?

RUSSIA
3. What can't be burned in fire, nor drowned in water?
4. What is it that no one can conquer?

Answers:

1. A chain.
2. A coconut.
3. Ice.
4. Sleep.

More Riddles

1. Why is it so cool at the ball park?
2. What did the tie say to the head?
3. Why do windows squeak?
4. Why does a thief never leave his house?
5. How do you drive a baby buggy?
6. How do you make antifreeze?
7. What did one candle say to another?

Answers:

1. There are so many fans there.
2. "You go on ahead; I'll just hang around here."
3. Because they have so many panes.
4. He doesn't want to be found out.
5. Tickle his feet.
6. Steal her shawl.
7. "Will you go out with me tonight?"

1. What country can't get enough to eat?
2. What country can you put on the table?
3. What country has the most fish?
4. What country helps you cook?
5. What is the coldest country in the world?
6. What's the first thing a farmer puts in his garden?

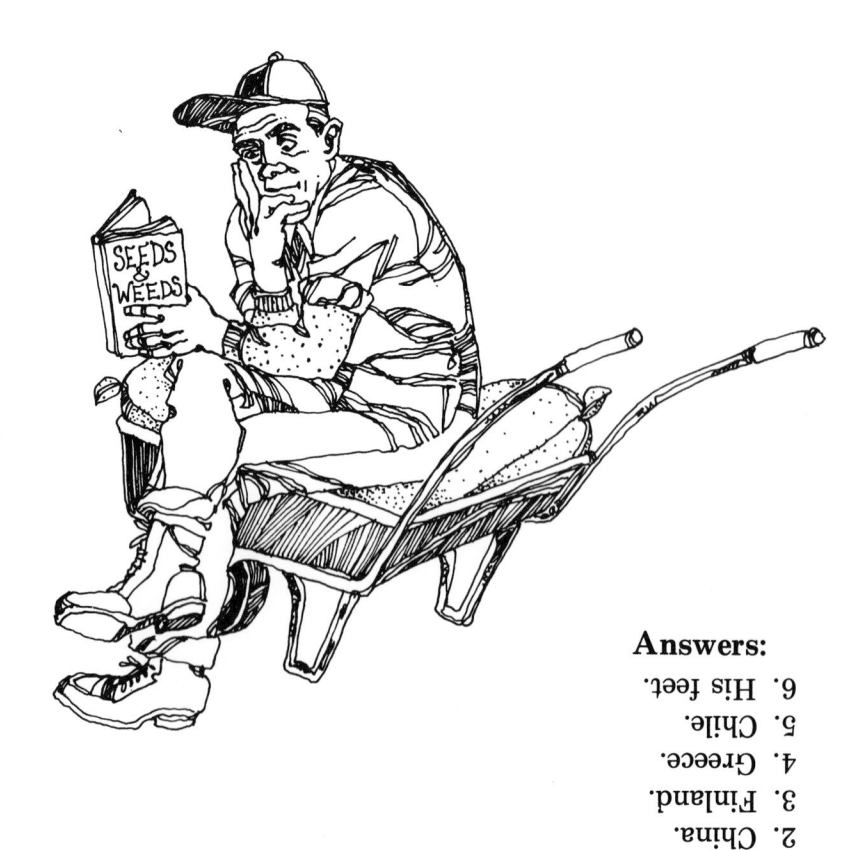

Answers:
1. Hungary.
2. China.
3. Finland.
4. Greece.
5. Chile.
6. His feet.

1. Why did the lawyer bring a ladder to the trial?

2. What word is always pronounced wrong?
3. Who should you call when your feet hurt?
4. What goes "HA HA HA PLOP"?
5. How do you make an egg roll?
6. Why is everyone in Moscow tired?
7. Why did the worker sit on a clock?

Answers:

1. He wanted to take his case to a higher court.
2. Wrong.
3. A toe truck.
4. Someone laughing his head off.
5. Push it down a hill.
6. Because everyone is Russian (rushing).
7. He wanted to work overtime.

1. How do you avoid falling hair?
2. Why did the doctor change jobs?
3. When is a letter not in the alphabet?
4. What did the umbrella say to the lady?
5. What do you call a pig that runs across the street and back?
6. Do spooks watch TV?
7. What goes "zub zub zub"?

Answers:

1. Step out of the way.
2. He lost his patients.
3. When it's in the post office.
4. "I've got you covered."
5. A dirty double crosser.
6. Yes, they have a ghost to ghost network.
7. A confused bee.

1. What is everyone in the world doing at the same time?
2. What letter can you drink?
3. What letter can you swim in?
4. Why can you see so much in England?
5. What disappears when you stand up?
6. What's the sleepiest mountain in the world?
7. If April showers bring May flowers, what do May flowers bring?

Answers:

1. Getting older.
2. T (tea).
3. C (sea).
4. Because it's an eye-land.
5. Your lap.
6. Mt. Everest (Ever-rest).
7. Pilgrims.

New Riddles

The riddles on pages 42-44 are originals. As far as the author knows, they have never before appeared in print. However, someone, somewhere, may have said something similar.

1. Why did the boy volunteer to carry the lamp?
2. How is a belt like a gangster?
3. What did the paper say to the pen?
4. Why did the new soldier put a lock on his foot locker?

Answers:
1. He heard there were light bulbs inside.
2. They both hold things up.
3. "Write on!"
4. There was private property inside.

1. Why did the man quit his job at the dry cleaners?
2. What is the fattest tree in the forest?
3. How do you make a banana split?
4. How is a cat like a light bulb?
5. How is a piano like a janitor?
6. Why did the guitar get upset?

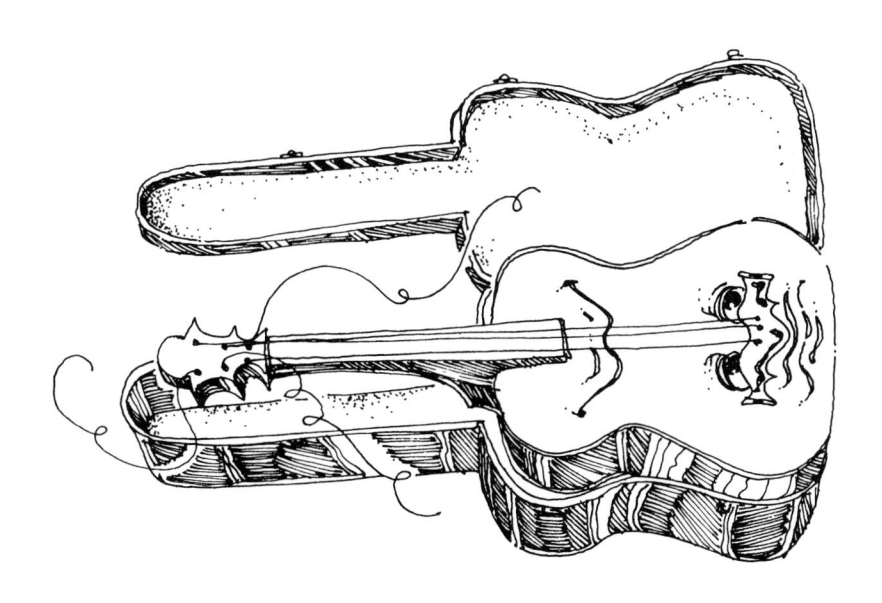

Answers:

1. He had a lot of hang ups.
2. The porky-pine.
3. Tell it a funny joke.
4. They both go out at night.
5. They both have a set of keys.
6. Everyone was picking on him.

1. Why did the baseball player retire early?
2. What did the log say to the match?
3. Where do old cows go?
4. What do you call a bird that becomes a majorette?
5. Where do pigs keep their money?
6. Why was the baby ant so confused?
7. Why did the boy hold down his book?

Answers:

1. He was afraid of bats.
2. "You burn me up."
3. To a moo-seum.
4. A twirly bird.
5. In people banks.
6. All of his uncles were ants.
7. Because it was a moving story.

Write Your Own Riddles

Riddles are like songs. People keep making up new ones. You may wonder how riddle-writing is done. Why don't *you* try? You may create some great new riddles that will amuse your friends . . . and the world!

To begin, remember that there are two important parts to a riddle—the question and the answer. In your question, you set up the situation. Your answer should be unexpected or surprising. Sometimes the surprise comes from using words that sound alike and look alike, but have different meanings.

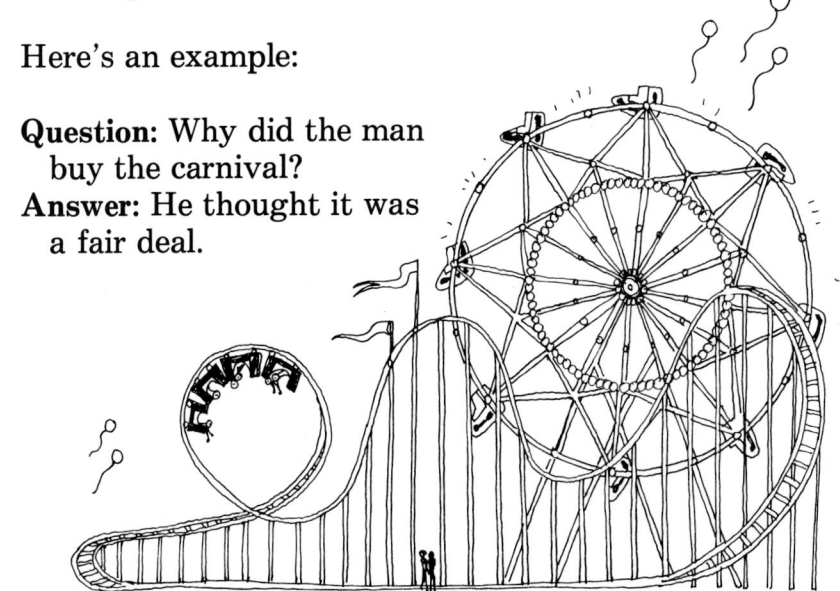

Here's an example:

Question: Why did the man buy the carnival?
Answer: He thought it was a fair deal.

The word "fair" is the key to the riddle. "Fair" can mean carnival or it can mean honest. You can probably think of other meanings for the word "fair." You could say someone had a fair complexion. You might use the word "fair" to mean average—neither good nor bad. You might say the weather was fair because there were no clouds in the sky. You might even use a word that is spelled differently but sounds like fair. For instance, you could build a riddle on "fare," which means the price you pay for something.

Sometimes a riddle simply offers an unexpected answer such as:

Question: Why did the chicken cross the road?
Answer: To get to the other side.

Here there is no play on words. The riddle leads you to think that the chicken had a good reason to cross the road. The simple answer is a surprise.

You have examined the parts of a riddle. Now consider the main types of riddles. This will help you get ready to write your own.

- Some riddles compare things. Comparison riddles ask how something is alike or different from something else. For instance:

Question: How is a book like a tree?
Answer: They both have leaves.

- Some riddles explain things.

Question: Why did the boy throw the clock out the window?
Answer: He wanted to see time fly.

- Other riddles tell someone how to do something. Here's an example:

Question: How do you make a car top?
Answer: Tep on the brake.

- Riddles can also describe something. Example:

Question: What runs through the woods but never gets tired?
Answer: A path.

- Perhaps the most common and easiest-to-write riddle asks, "What is it?" Take a look at this one:

Question: What are the smartest animals in the sea?
Answer: Fish. They go around in schools.

There are many kinds of riddles. The examples above can get you started. Don't be afraid to use your imagination. And that brings us to our last riddle—

Question: What country do all riddles come from?
Answer: Why, the imagine nation, of course!

T 004351